COACH'S PLAN

The Personal Productivity System That Changed My Life

MIKE KAVANAGH

Coach's Plan: The Personal Productivity System That Changed My Life

Copyright © 2021 by Mike Kavanagh

All rights reserved under International and Pan-American Copyright Conventions. No part of this book may be reproduced in any form or by any means, electronic or mechanical, including photocopying, recording, or by any information storage and retrieval system, without permission in writing from the author, except in the case of brief quotations embodied in critical articles and reviews.

ISBN: 9798477816705

Table of Contents

Table of Contents iii

How Do You Start? 5

The Epiphany 11

Your Two Selves 15

Retire the Player-Coach 19

Coach's Plan: The Theory 23

Coach's Plan: The Practice 31

Trust Coach's Plan 49

You, The All-Star 69

Uncommon Acknowledgments 71

How Do You Start?

I'm terrible at starting books. I sit with a blank page before me, and I fumble.

How you kick off your book is very important. That's what the experts say. The first few pages are how a person determines if they want to read on. They need to pack a punch.

Instead, what usually happens is the blank page punches me, repeatedly, in the face.

So, there it was…that was it. That was my weak open. No powerful story. Nothing resembling a hook whatsoever. Just a moment of honesty.

I'm terrible at starting books.

And there are lots of other things I'm terrible at too. Important things. Things that matter a ton to a person who left the financially stable, tried-and-true path of being a corporate executive to start from scratch as a solopreneur doing what he loves…as the sole breadwinner with a wife and two young kids to support…and with limited savings to keep the family afloat.

Here are some of the things it's not good to be terrible at when you set out on your own as an entrepreneur, or when you aspire to succeed in any realm for that matter.

It's not good to be terrible at avoiding procrastination. It's not good to be terrible at breaking bad habits. It's not good to be terrible at networking, or making cold calls, or selling, or doing anything that falls under the umbrella of self-promotion.

It's not good to be terrible at these things, or a lot of other important things I'm terrible at as judged by any of the extra-forgiving objective measures out there.

But something happened to me on my journey. I had an epiphany, and it changed everything.

My epiphany was a specific realization about myself. The moment of insight also came paired with a practical hack—a self-hack.

Let me be clear about something. Prior to this epiphany, the word "hack" never applied to me or my life, except perhaps in describing me on a golf course, or me with an upper respiratory infection.

But life-hacking? No ma'am, no sir.

In fact, I have an allergy to that sort of thing. I break out in hives the minute somebody tries to sell me on some big promise.

It's not that I'm opposed to life-hacks as a concept. I love a good shortcut if it genuinely saves me time, energy, headache, or heartache. I fully embrace techniques if they truly improve the quality of my life, my productivity, or my contribution to the world at large.

And there are many examples of techniques that have had such effects on my life.

It's just that most of the promises out there turn out to be garbage. People love to try to sell us big promises that are the supposed answer to all our problems—especially people who don't have anything worth selling us. Those people really seem to need the money.

And here I come along, about to tell you I have something that might help you in some incredible ways.

It might be the way to overcome your procrastination and become more productive than you've ever been. It might be the thing that triggers you to follow through with a daily exercise routine when you've fallen off the fitness wagon. It might help you finally kick your sugar habit. It might be the key that allows you to go from aspiring author to writing and releasing two books in nine months. It might be the thing that enables you to launch an entirely new business, without sacrificing sleep and still having ample quality time for your important relationships. It might even do all these things at the same time.

It might. It might not.

I say *it might* because it did for me. Genuinely. Every one of those examples I just rattled off—every single one of those happened in my life after my epiphany.

I say *it might not* because I'm a realist. Not everyone is ready to try something new, nor does everyone follow through.

I say *it might* because one of the hats I wear is as a mind-body trainer, teaching meditation and breathwork, coaching fitness, and as a behavior change specialist. I know how significant personal transformations can be. I've seen some big ones.

I say *it might not* because we're all human, and no method is a silver bullet for overcoming our humanity, thankfully. You'd be a very boring and uninteresting human if you were perfect.

In fact, let me extend that last point further.

A moment ago, I rattled off many positive outcomes I experienced after my epiphany. Some of those were aspirations I harbored for years but couldn't turn into reality. Then this method came along for me, and I watched as those aspirations became my lived experience. I witnessed first-hand how powerful employing this method was for me.

Yet, despite experiencing these fruits, my commitment to the method hasn't been one hundred percent.

How about them apples?

That's right. I'm admitting to you that even the very thing I'm "pitching" to you right now—this method that I believe was and is a complete game changer in my life—I don't always use it.

Because I'm human.

Nobody's perfect. Nor is any method perfect.

And by the way, any so-called expert of who-knows-what who gives you the impression they're one hundred percent *on it* with respect to anything is probably full of it. That's one of those things that triggers my allergy.

Truth be told, I'm not actually pitching you anything. I used that word for effect. I'm just sharing. I want to help people. I share what I think has the potential to help. Whether it does or doesn't help, that's not for me to decide. I focus on my intention and my personal process, and I leave the rest to unfold as it will.

I'd also like to clarify something else I said earlier. I referred to this thing I'm about to share as a "self-hack." I used the word "hack" because it did feel like this was a reprogramming or an end-around of my normal operating system.

But hack makes it sound like a quick and easy shortcut to results. That's not what this is. It's more of a "method," a "process," or a "system."

Enough with the preamble. Let's cut to the chase.

Here's my story in a nutshell:

Not too long ago, I set out on an entrepreneurial path and spent a bunch of months spinning my wheels, procrastinating, getting stuck in self-doubt, and struggling with mediocre productivity.

Then, my epiphany happened, which came paired with a method I employed in my life that I refer to as "Coach's Plan."

As soon as I implemented Coach's Plan, incredible things happened to me—the things I described earlier.

That sounds like a sales pitch. But let me make myself extremely clear:

I *never* had any intent on writing a book on personal productivity. That's never been my schtick.

But I feel compelled to share this because of the impact it had on my life—not only with respect to my personal productivity, but also with personal change more broadly. I know this can help other people, too.

There's simply no way I'm unique when it comes to this stuff. If this empowered me the way it did, it has the potential to empower at least one other human being out there to do incredible things.

I hope that's you.

So, I'm making some predictions right here, right now:

I fully expect some people to implement Coach's Plan with revolutionary results (during those times they follow through with it). These people will accomplish amazing things, and their confidence and all-around mojo will soar.

I expect others to come away feeling like it missed the mark for them, or they won't bother putting it into practice in their life. That's just how it is with everything. Nothing is for everybody.

Some people will find real insight in here and run with it. Others will scratch their heads and ask, "That's it? But it's so basic," or, "It's similar to XYZ," and then they'll throw tomatoes at me.

But here's the deal:

I follow Coach's Plan, and it's telling me to push this little manual for personal change out into the world, come what may.

Coach's Plan is my spin on an approach to overcoming age-old human problems that nearly all of us struggle to address. And it's completely authentic—it came into my life spontaneously, I implemented it, and it worked for me.

So, let's get to it. Without further ado, the short book with a terrible opener that I never expected to write is about to get down to business.

The Epiphany

Remember that big epiphany I mentioned? Let me tell you about it.

I was in the middle of a significant career transition. After ten years as a consultant and advisor to senior executives of Fortune 500 companies and several years in corporate leadership roles, including as a C-level executive, I experienced a first in my life:

My first layoff. Private equity induced.

It hadn't exactly been a smooth ride in the couple of years leading up to that moment, so I was ready for a change. But I wasn't ready to charge down a new path because of the *somewhat* unexpected nature of the transition. There was a lot I still needed to figure out.

Here's what I knew:

I knew I wanted to take a shot at something entrepreneurial, and I wanted it to incorporate my deepest personal passions, including coaching/teaching/training, writing, and public speaking in the realm of mind-body performance. I had been coaching and teaching mental training, meditation, breathwork, fitness, and behavior change on the side for about a decade, but never had the audacity to turn it into a central part of my livelihood.

THE EPIPHANY

Here's what I didn't know:

I didn't know exactly how I should go about doing this. There were lots of forms it could potentially take. I needed to pick a direction.

So, I set out down a path I thought of as my Plan A. I made some early progress and experienced some wins. But early on, my progress was stymied. It slowed to a crawl.

There were several factors. Some were external and understandable, like significant world events.

But most were mental.

The long and short of it was that I found myself stuck in a strange self-created holding pattern, where I kept myself plenty busy but didn't seem to be accomplishing anything substantial.

During this period, I procrastinated. I avoided critical, uncomfortable tasks like cold-calling and selling in favor of any other tasks, even if they were trivial.

Soon, I started paying the price.

My output was too low. My savings were lower. I felt my dreams slipping away.

Worse than that, my confidence tanked. After all, I knew I wasn't doing the things I should be doing. It's one thing to give it your all and fail. It's another thing to fail to give it your all.

I began seriously doubting if I had what it took to be successful pursuing this path I felt called to pursue.

And even worse than that, I began feeling like a fraud.

Why?

Do you want mental training advice from a person who can't get out of his own self-doubt spiral, or fitness advice from a guy who can't string together more than a workout or two a week, or nutrition advice from a guy who is housing copious quantities of cookies and ice cream every night, or business consulting from a person whose own business isn't achieving liftoff?

Neither do I.

There are certain professions where it's understandable that the shoemaker's son—and the shoemaker himself—goes barefoot.

I don't think mine is one of them. Walk the talk. You don't have to be perfect. But live it to the best of your ability.

Setting all that aside, I also just wanted my normal sense of balance and mojo back. I wanted mental, physical, and financial health.

Instead, I felt like I was letting myself and my family down.

Amid this period, I laid in bed contemplating the rut I found myself in. I did this most nights. Usually, I spent the time making promises to myself about what I would accomplish the next day—promises I would break the next day to complete the vicious cycle.

One night, as I was reflecting on my pattern, I had an internal conversation with myself.

"Mike, you know what you need to do. If you were coaching yourself as a client, you know what you would encourage him to do to help him through this. So, why don't you put your coaching hat on and coach yourself?"

"Sure, Mike, that's true. I know what I *should* do. But that's not my problem. My problem is I'm not doing it, and I don't really know why. I'm stuck. I'm stagnant. There's obviously some kind of inner block in me. It's probably fear of some sort. But I don't seem to know how to break through it."

"Okay, Mike, but is that really unique? Wouldn't you agree that's what most of the people you work with are actually struggling with? Deep down, most of the time, they know what they should do. Their problem isn't really a lack of knowledge. Their problem is with how to break through their current point of stagnation and get some momentum."

"Hmmm…that's true. Mike, you're making some sense. But you usually make sense at night after reflecting on what you didn't do right that day. The problem is that tomorrow rolls around, and it doesn't translate into action."

"That's exactly my point, Mike. Coach yourself right now on this specific problem. What could you do, right now, to break through this specific problem you face? You know what you need to do, but you're not doing it when tomorrow rolls around. There's your problem. What haven't you tried yet that you could try to address that problem?"

BING!

That was the inner lightbulb turning on. Although, if I'm to get my onomatopoeia right, it was more of a *BAAAAMMMM*.

In a flash, a self-hack/method/system materialized out of nothing. I *knew* what I needed to do. I went downstairs and set the wheels in motion.

Thus began a total shift that eventually became these words I'm sharing with you now.

Your Two Selves

"My diet starts tomorrow," we say as we finish off the piece of chocolate cake.

"I'll make those sales calls tomorrow," we say when our lack of motivation has gotten the better of us.

"I'll get back to the gym on Monday," we say at that precise point when we've given up our hopes of squeezing in a workout that day.

"I'll take a hiatus from drinking after the party this weekend," we say, pushing our aspiration to an ambiguous future date that we're likely to push off again by the time it arrives.

You have two selves. Arguably, you have more than two. But for this metaphor, we're sticking to two.

One You is wise. One You knows what's best. One You can reflect on what you're doing well and where you're missing the mark, and can accurately diagnose the good, the bad, and the ugly.

If that You were truly in charge all the time, you would knock it out of the park in almost every area of your life.

Forget accruing more knowledge or expertise for a second. If you just took what you know right now about how to live your best life—how to optimize your health, how to be successful and productive, how to maximize your mental and emotional well-being, and you lived all of *that*… would you or would you not be a regular superhero?

You would crush it and your mojo would be off the charts all the time.

But that's not what happens. Because that You who knows isn't always in charge. For most of us, that You who knows is rarely in charge. Instead, that You is more like Statler and Waldorf, the two Muppets in the theater balcony heaving insults at whatever show they're watching.

The You who shows up on the field often forgets the plays the other You drew up in your best moments of lucidity. The You who shows up on the field is a mixed bag, capable of moments and periods of enlightened action and superstar results, as well as utterly disappointing performances that are many levels below your full potential.

This is true for all of us. It's called being human.

Even all-stars have their weak moments and their low phases. The only difference between all-stars and everyone else is the amount of time they spend in each of the various levels of their potential.

Here is the truth I saw on the night of my epiphany regarding my two selves:

Nighttime Mike is clear and generally on-point about what Next-Day Mike should do to have an outstanding day.

Next-Day Mike is highly prone to breaking Nighttime Mike's promises and prefers to follow his own whims and moods.

Nighttime Mike is ready to delay gratification and play the long game if that's what's likely to yield better results in the end.

Next-Day Mike is impulsive and easily swallowed up by short-term urges.

Nighttime Mike's motivation for crushing it in life is high. But it's theoretical.

Next-Day Mike's motivation ebbs and flows. But it's what dictates Mike's actual results in life.

To sum all of this up…

Nighttime Mike has the makings of a great coach. But he's not the one on the field.

Next-Day Mike is an unreliable coach to himself, and his performance on the field oscillates significantly depending on the day.

The night of the epiphany, a question came to me:

What if I embraced the reality of these two selves and found a way to harness the powers each of them have?

If that sounds ambiguous, it will become clear soon.

Retire the Player-Coach

When most of us get down to business in daily life, we become the player-coach.

By "get down to business," I'm talking about when you switch into productive mode in your personal or professional life and work to accomplish any of the goals or tasks you set for yourself for the day.

Exercising. Running errands. Making work calls. Completing work deliverables.

By "player-coach," I mean exactly what that means in any other domain—you're the player and you're the coach. The player side of you is the doer. It's the executor. The coach side of you sets your plan, determines your schedule, and makes higher order decisions.

Here's the crux of the productivity and habit-change challenges most of us face as human beings:

Throughout the day, you are confronted with decision points.

Should I tackle these emails right now, or should I make that call? Should I work out now or later? Should I eat a salad for lunch, or should I have what I really feel like eating? I'm slowing down on this work task... should I keep going until I finish, or should I switch and come back to it during my next block of free time this afternoon?

At each one of these points, the player-coach makes a choice.

What determines which decision you make?

Innumerable conscious and sub-conscious drivers.

Logical evaluation. Your motivation levels. Your energy levels. Your intuition. Your conscious determination of what's best. Your mood. Your willpower. Your stress levels.

Your decision is dictated by whatever combination of drivers is strongest in the moment.

So, within the player-coach metaphor, *who* determines your decision?

Sometimes it's the player. Sometimes it's the coach. Sometimes it's happenstance.

I think you see the issue. The factors determining whether a given decision is a good choice or a poor choice in retrospect are unlikely to be consistently tuned for optimal decision-making.

I think you *feel* the issue, too, don't you?

Who doesn't? Our productivity levels ebb and flow quite a lot. So does the degree to which we follow through with our many goals and aspirations.

That's because the level of our goal-achievement and overall productivity is the direct result of summing up all those tiny little decisions we're making along the way.

Most of us believe this just is how it is. It's part of being a human.

I certainly did. And of course, there's truth to it.

But what most of us don't realize is that our default tendency is to approach this issue in the wrong way.

RETIRE THE PLAYER-COACH

We put the onus of responsibility on the player-coach in the moment.

For example, to increase the quality and quantity of our work output in any given hour, we focus on how we can improve our motivation levels, or how we can fight procrastination.

Or here's another example. To improve the quality of our dietary choices, we focus on how we can increase our discipline and our willpower.

In other words, we try to find ways to become a better player-coach in the moment.

It turns out there is a far better approach.

Retire the player-coach.

That's right. Thank the player-coach for all their solid effort over the years and bid them a fond farewell. You can retire their jersey if you'd like. They've gotten you this far.

But your team is under new management, and management runs things differently.

The way management runs things is to embrace your two selves and what each of them does best, to articulate clear roles for each self, and to give each of them a defined set of responsibilities.

To begin with, management has hired a new coach. That coach knows their place, and it isn't on the field... it's on the sidelines doing what coaches do best.

Management has also hired a new player. That player knows their place as well, and it's exclusively on the field, following Coach's Plan.

Coach's Plan: The Theory

First, I want to congratulate you for getting hired for such a prestigious role.

Coaching can be a tough job. The coach is the one watching the videos after every game and analyzing what went right and what went wrong. The coach is the one who tries new things in constant pursuit of *better*, even though some of those experiments fail. When things don't go well, the coach takes a lot of heat.

But a coach is an expert in crafting a game plan that acknowledges a player's weaknesses and draws the best out of a player to drive superior results. When that's happening, it's a rewarding role indeed.

I also want to congratulate you for getting signed to the team as the all-star player.

The player's role comes with its own unique characteristics and challenges. The player is the one who puts in the training hours, showing up day in and day out regardless of how they feel.

It's rewarding as well, because just like professional athletes, few people in the world can do what an all-star player does in the Coach's Plan system. The player becomes a true master of being in the moment, shutting out external and internal noise, and channeling their focus into stellar performance.

Is the player always on fire, executing at peak performance and intensity levels? Of course not. But the more you train in showing up to the game ready to switch into the mode of the true professional, the more wins you bank, and the more success begets success.

This delineation of roles is one of the core secrets to the power of Coach's Plan.

The Coach *builds the plan*. The player *executes the plan*.

In effect, what this means is that you are removing decision power from the You who shows up to do the *work*—the sometimes unreliable You who previously made game-time choices that were heavily influenced by mood, motivation, energy, willpower, and all sorts of other sub-optimal factors.

Showing up to do the work doesn't simply mean professional work, it encompasses any personal or professional goal you have for a given day that requires effort and is at risk of not happening because of any of the sub-optimal factors that influence our decisions and actions. Your goals may be tasks you want to complete, habits you want to form or break, or even a mentality you wish to embody.

As for the transfer of decision power, the idea is to remove decision rights from the You who shows up to do the work to the maximum degree that's possible. I'll address some of the nuances of how to do this when we move from theory to practical implementation.

The key point is that, when you show up for game time, you become the all-star player who is focused on one thing and one thing alone: execution.

This is a learned skill. It may feel awkward or uncomfortable at first. Most of us have never even contemplated living a day entirely as the executors of somebody else's wishes, even if those wishes came from ourselves the day before.

Let's slide into a different metaphor for a moment.

Imagine living a day as the perfect soldier. Imagine you are somebody who follows the plan laid out for you without succumbing to your temptation to bend those plans on the margin because of your momentary preferences, and without internally griping about those plans. Imagine placing complete and total trust in the general's battle plan because you know from experience that the general's plans are deserving of that level of trust.

How does that sound?

If it doesn't sound great, I understand. That's what I thought too.

But after experimenting with this approach, what I discovered surprised me.

First, going about my daily business in this way freed a tremendous amount of psychic energy. Few of us realize how much energy we burn making hundreds of tiny decisions throughout the day, most of which can be placed on autopilot in the form of following a well-crafted plan.

Likewise, few of us realize how much energy we burn throughout the day investing in a mental narrative about our experience. This includes inner complaints we have when we're trying to push ourselves to do something we'd rather not be doing. It also includes the guilt, shame, and anxiety that show up when we're procrastinating or when we're not following through on one of the goals we set for ourselves.

Following Coach's Plan removed a ton of this mental energy burn from the first day I started using it.

My second surprising finding was this:

Going about my daily business in this way gave me tremendous energy and yielded extraordinary output.

We've all had those days when we're crushing it, powering through task after task and accomplishing goal after goal. The satisfaction and sense of accomplishment is potent and energizing.

My third surprising finding was that going about my daily business in this way did not have many of the downsides I predicted.

I thought asking myself to go about things in this way was the equivalent of asking myself to spend my day as a mindless robot, just chipping away at tasks. I was convinced this couldn't possibly be a satisfying way to live my day. I also worried that by removing my intelligent reflection and corresponding adjustments in the moment, my results might suffer.

I was wrong on both counts.

My satisfaction went up because of a point I made earlier. The real source of psychological struggle and strife is the mental narrative you overlay on your experience. When you learn to follow Coach's Plan, so much of this mental overlay gets quieted. I'll explain this more as we get deeper into what Coach's Plan is and how to implement it.

My productivity also went up *without* my usual reflection and game-time adjustments throughout the day. This is because, when you adjust a solid plan in the moment, you tend to make more bad adjustments than you do good ones.

The reason for this turns out to be obvious: your adjustments are heavily influenced by how you feel in the moment.

I'm tired. I'll work out later.

I have free time this afternoon. I'll wait to make that difficult call until then.

You get the picture. By allowing game-time adjustments, you invite subtle urges and desires that aren't in your best interest to enter the decision-making equation.

Yes, sometimes you are faced with a moment where a potential game-time adjustment is clearly a positive change to make, and it feels foolish to ignore it. The problem is that by inviting game-time adjustments, you allow *all* of them in—good and bad—and the aggregate result is a net negative.

Keep in mind that you aren't cutting out intelligent adjustments entirely when you follow Coach's Plan. You simply defer them to the end of the day, after execution for the day is complete.

I wanted to share all this mental pushback I personally experienced because I'm unlikely to be the only one with these sorts of thoughts. Implementing a system like this runs counter to how many of us have been conditioned.

In fact, when this system first came to me, I remember thinking, "This is crazy. Is there any way it'll really work? It's almost like I'm treating Next-Day Mike like a child. There's no way Next-Day Mike will follow this. He'll rebel. He'll be the prima-donna-all-star athlete who has to do things his way."

This reminds me of a scene in the movie *Moneyball* where the general manager, Billy Beane, approaches one of his players in batting practice to convince him to stop swinging at so many pitches and follow the team's new strategy, which is all about taking more walks and simply getting on base. This notion runs counter to the athlete's desire to take big swings, get hits and homeruns, and be the star. But ultimately, he gets on board with the plan, and the team's results speak for themselves.

In truth, the crazy idea behind Coach's Plan isn't about treating Next-Day Mike like a child at all. It's about trusting Next-Day Mike to be a true professional and giving him a new set of tools to reach his full potential.

When the idea behind Coach's Plan first came to me, I never envisioned it as a system I would follow beyond a day or two. I just wanted a day or two of discipline to break myself out of a lull and get some momentum.

I never realized how powerful this separation of roles is when it comes to mastering each respective role. Nor did I anticipate how powerful you become when you marry these independent roles in the way I describe in the next chapter.

But now it seems obvious.

Imagine I gave you two tasks to complete today.

Your first task: Place 1000 stamps on 1000 envelopes.

Your second task: Write a 1000-word article on the fall of the Roman Empire using internet research. But no Wiki, you cheater.

Ready. Set. Go!

Wait, wait. I forgot to tell you… you can only type one word at a time before you must stop to place a stamp on an envelope, and vice versa.

One stamp, one word, back and forth until completion.

By the way, I gave this same task to my friend Liz, but she can do things in whatever order she wants. And this is a race. And quality matters, too.

Go!

My money is on Liz, no offense. If I were in this race, I'd rather be Liz. I'm not saying I'd enjoy placing hundreds of stamps at a time on envelopes, but I'm pretty sure I'd get into a rhythm, and my first 20 stamp placements would go a lot slower than, say, stamps 100 to 120.

My point isn't to caution you about the woes of multi-tasking. Any time you step into a role where there is a clear division of labor, you're more efficient. Your learning on that task accelerates as well, because of your focus and clarity of purpose.

I lived an interesting example of this when one of my teams changed the way we ran our interview and hiring process and began dividing up the roles each of us played in the process.

A couple of people focused primarily on probing a candidate's background experience and competency for the job itself. Another couple of people focused on assessing character-related qualities. And another couple of people focused on the candidate's culture fit.

Previously, everyone probed a little bit of everything. But once each of us put on our assigned hats and spent the bulk of our time in our elected area, we became much more skilled at evaluating that area. And when we combined our collective views, we tended to arrive at better decisions. The quality of our hiring improved.

When you embrace Coach's Plan, you still wear the same hats you did before. You just don't wear them all at once. And you become so much more effective at each of the roles you play.

You have an amazing coach in you.

You also have an amazing player in you.

Let's put them to work.

Coach's Plan: The Practice

It's time to put Coach's Plan into practice. It's very simple. But don't let its simplicity fool you. There is tremendous power in simplicity. And we'll get to the subtleties soon enough.

Here's how Coach's Plan works.

At the end of your day, you are going to sit down as Coach and write a plan for the next day. The end of your day can be the end of your workday, or it can be in the evening. You can write your plan digitally or in a paper notebook. It's worth experimenting with both options to see what works best for you. You can also download a free printable pdf template at www.mikekav.com/books to save yourself a step.

When I sit down as Coach, the whole process takes me 15 to 30 minutes.

Let's talk about the plan. Your plan is going to be divided into several sections:

- Goals
- Workout
- To Do
- Schedule

- Ideas/Notes
- Process Observations
- Results
- Tomorrow

Let's dive into each section one-by-one.

Goals

The Goals section is the space for you to include the little personal victories you want to achieve tomorrow that aren't clearly defined tasks you could otherwise easily incorporate into your Schedule section.

"Follow Coach's Plan to the letter" is one example.

Another example is something you want to successfully *not* do, like a habit you aspire to break.

When I first implemented Coach's Plan, I was a sugar fiend and was eating cookies and ice cream every night. Early on, I included "No sugar," or "No dessert" as a goal.

I was also entrenched in a habit of consuming too much media. I included "No media" as a goal.

I recommend framing goals with positive wording if you can, since we tend to have greater success following a "do this" rather than a "don't do this."

In my own case, "no dessert" became "Cereal/fruit for dessert" while I weaned. My "no media" goal became "Successful media fast."

These real examples did not show up on my list of goals every day—more on that later.

Workout

Movement of any kind is critical to you being the best version of yourself. Exercise is one of the single biggest energy and mood boosters known to humanity.

You'll soon find out that your follow-through on any task or goal increases exponentially when you write things down and implement the Coach's Plan approach. You also remove the guesswork for Next-Day You when Coach has written the workout plan for you the previous day.

Here's an example for the workout section:

20 push-ups | 20 air squats | 1 minute rest | Repeat until time runs out.

Here's another example of what might fit in the Workout section:

Go for a 30-minute walk.

I think you get the picture. Your workout can be doing a video or a class, it can be getting some outdoor activity, it can be anything at all that you wish. It doesn't have to be something we traditionally think of as exercise. Just get your body moving. That's the point.

"But Mike, really? Include a workout section every day? You're crazy! There's no way I can fit in a workout every single day."

You're jumping to conclusions, my friend.

Include the section every day, and when you're taking a day off, you can lean on my final example workout. It's one of my absolute favorites when I've earned it:

Rest day.

To Do

Your To Do section is the list of tasks you want to accomplish tomorrow.

Go to the grocery store. Finish deliverable XYZ. Do my taxes.

Here is an important point about your To Do section:

This is your aspirational list of tasks *for the next day*. It's not your entire To Do list. It's demoralizing to constantly look at absolutely every undone thing you need to accomplish in the coming days, weeks, and months.

Keep your master list in another location, and port over an achievable number of tasks for tomorrow. That's it.

Better still, separate this achievable list into two categories. For the purposes of this illustration, I am calling the categories "Primary" and "If there's time." You can use whatever descriptions you want.

Most people overestimate how much they can get done in a day. Then, they judge their daily output based on their misguided expectations, and they feel defeated when they come up short, even though, objectively, they may have had a highly productive day.

I have perfectionist tendencies, so my trick is that my "Primary" category could just as accurately be labeled: "The bare minimum, absolute must-dos that keep me from destroying relationships or tanking my livelihood."

Let me explain.

If you really look at what you absolutely must accomplish on any given day, the truth is often much more forgiving than your self-judging-idealistic-inner-overachiever is willing to admit. (This point applies to anyone who has one of those self-judging-idealistic-inner-overachievers in them.)

So, be honest about what is truly critical to get done. You don't have to stop there, and if you follow Coach's Plan, you won't. But this is a critical reframe that positions you for success and mental well-being.

It might sound funny to you that I'm including this seemingly anti-productivity message in a book about a personal process for maximizing productivity and catalyzing personal change, but I've come to see how important it is. Biting off more than you can chew is a productivity killer.

Some days, I have one thing in my primary To Do column. Occasionally, *every* task falls into the "If there's time" category.

The beautiful thing about Coach's Plan is that, over time, you hone your planning faculties, and your plans become more realistic. You become far more effective at anticipating how much you can accomplish in a day.

How?

You owe part of that prowess to the next section.

Schedule

When you employ Coach's Plan, you schedule every minute of your productive hours.

Hold on. Before I lose you, please hear me out.

If you aren't somebody who schedules your time like this, and you think, "There's no way I'm going to do *that*," you're in good company, because that's exactly where I was before all this came into my life.

But the Schedule section is at the core of what enables the division of responsibility between Coach and Player that we discussed earlier. This is what allows you to switch off big parts of your psyche, to surrender to a beautiful plan that you yourself created for the Next-Day version of you, and to learn just how much mojo comes from getting into the flow of executing a wonderfully crafted plan.

I will share some of the secrets of a beautiful, mojo-filled plan with you shortly. So, I'm asking you to trust me for now, or at least to hold your skepticism for the moment.

When I sit down as Coach and create a plan, I schedule the moment I wake up to the moment my workday is complete in varying levels of detail. Here is an actual example of one of my schedules… one of the ones that makes me look good:

- 6:00 – 6:45 Workout
- 6:45 – 7:15 Meditate, have coffee
- 7:15 – 8:00 Make kids breakfast, eat, coffee
- 8:00 – 8:30 Shower/get ready
- 8:30 – 9:30 Work on book
- 9:30 – 10:30 Consulting - call with team
- 10:30 – 10:45 Break, walk outside
- 10:45 – 11:45 Consulting - work on presentation
- 11:45 – 12:30 Lunch
- 12:30 – 1:30 Cold calls/cold emails
- 1:30 – 2:30 Consulting - call with client
- 2:30 – 3:00 Break - walk outside
- 3:00 – 4:30 Email, To Do
- 4:30 – 5:00 Coach's Plan for tomorrow

For a "Workout" slot like the one above, Next-Day Mike simply follows the workout Coach laid out the day before.

For my "Email, To Do," section, Next-Day Mike checks and responds to email, and chips away at the To Do list Coach established for him, including tasks that were not explicitly scheduled with a separate block of time.

On this example day, I assumed that 90 minutes was enough to accomplish my "Primary" tasks and stay reasonably on top of email.

I'll spare you alternative versions of the schedule, including the ones that make me look bad, but I want to mention a couple things.

I often go through periods where I don't wake up at a set time. But I usually know around when I'm likely to wake up, so I build the schedule around a conservative guess and bake in some flexibility. During those periods, my first item might look like this:

? – 7:30 Kids, coffee, breakfast

After that, I resume with a normal schedule.

The other callout I'd like to make has to do with email. I do not check email periodically throughout the day. If I need to stay more on top of email than the example I included above, I schedule it. If I'm in an email-heavy phase, I might include 30 minutes of email mid-morning, 30 minutes in the early afternoon, and a larger block of time toward the end of the day to catch up.

I strongly recommend you follow this approach of scheduling time for email and similar forms of communication. We'll come back to this, but part of the power of Coach's Plan comes from eliminating as many distractions as possible.

Will Next-Day You get hit with surprises?

Of course.

Will Next-Day You need to adjust your schedule on the fly?

Of course.

We'll talk about how to do that shortly. For now, remember this:

Stick to the plan to the best of your ability. Execute like a pro.

Ideas/Notes

Coach leaves this section blank.

This section is meant for Next-Day You to capture any great idea you have throughout the day, or anything you don't want to forget.

The primary purpose of this section is to avoid getting pulled away from what you're doing when certain ideas or inputs come into your awareness.

The moment you have thoughts like, "Oh, I forgot this…" or "Oh, that's brilliant, I should really…" your job is to write them down, then go back to the task at hand. You can come back to these items during a To Do block of your schedule, during a Coach's Plan block, or at the end of your day.

One of the beautiful things about Coach's Plan that you are likely to experience is a high degree of creativity and insight. It's satisfying to watch as you populate this section with moments of genius throughout the day.

That's just how it is when you get into the groove of Coach's Plan. You free up so much of the intelligence that was previously bound up in making choices about how you spend your time, as well as other forms of unnecessary decision swirl and mental narrative.

The result is sharpened thinking and frequent visitation by unexpected insights and breakthroughs.

Process Observations

Coach leaves this section blank as well.

This section is where Next-Day You captures any specific idea, observation, or insight you have about Coach's Plan itself.

In other words, this is where you document observations about what's working and what isn't with your plan so Coach can get better at planning. Think of this as the feedback loop.

You didn't allot enough time for email or administrative tasks? Note that. Now Coach knows.

You scheduled a critical, mentally intense task during your afternoon energy slump? Note that. Now Coach knows.

Herein lies the power of this system for productivity and personal change. Your personal process becomes *adaptive*. You begin to observe at a micro level what works best for you, the executor.

Coach's Plan allows you to run small experiments with documented results. It's all right there for you on paper, or digitally as the case may be. You have written evidence of what you do that yields the best outcomes in terms of your productivity and your daily well-being.

I learned so much about myself when I implemented this in my life—subtle things that allowed me to make small changes with huge impact.

For example, I became incredibly mindful of my rhythms and my biology, and I understood the cause and effect behind my periods of high and low energy with a precision I never had before. This allowed me to make adjustments that yielded tremendous energy.

For example, I learned that delaying having coffee until just before getting to work was an incredible boost to my morning output.

I learned that scheduling 30 minutes for a walk at 2:30 allowed me to eliminate most of my typical afternoon slumps.

I compared the impact of carbohydrate-rich lunches and no-carb lunches on my afternoon energy levels, and I nearly eliminated energy slumps altogether.

I witnessed how much better my results were on days when I scheduled breaks, compared with days where I tried to forego breaks and cram too much in.

I saw the unproductive angst that came when I created schedules requiring a hurried pace. I made simple changes, like giving myself 40 minutes for lunch instead of 30 minutes.

In addition to observations about my biology, I learned valuable things related to the content of my work.

One example of this took the form of a new mantra for me regarding writing and content creation projects:

Only forward.

Whenever I was creating a first draft of anything, I stopped allowing myself to go backward to make changes along the way. I saw how much time I usually spent editing and cleaning things up as I went. Many of these edits became moot, because once I had a full draft, I typically slashed big swaths of what I created anyway. By only moving forward, I saved time, increased my output, and enjoyed the creation process more.

I also began building plans that included more variety in the schedule. For tasks where it was appropriate to do this, I broke them up into two or three chunks throughout the day and included very different tasks in between. This kept my days fresh and improved my outlook.

Related to this, I spread small, focused periods of doing uncomfortable tasks amid a variety of palatable tasks, which made me more likely to follow through on the hard things. By not turning such tasks into long slogs, and by having a defined endpoint with something to look forward to immediately afterward, my execution of difficult tasks went up and my days became more enjoyable.

Because of these changes and many other examples, my results improved in dramatic ways. I know this is an objectively true statement because my results were documented every day in the next section.

Results

This is another section Coach leaves blank for Next-Day You to fill in. This is the section where you log your accomplishments for the day.

What did you achieve?

I completed X. This is how far I got on task Y.

Simple.

One of the side-benefits of employing the Coach's Plan system is that you have a documented history of what you did and what you accomplished in the form of the Schedule and Results sections. This can be a very valuable resource for all sorts of things.

I have used Coach's Plan as a simple memory aid: "When did I have that meeting?" "What did I do last Friday?"

I have used it to retrospectively track how much time I typically spend on certain tasks or projects. Coach's Plan keeps me honest.

I have even used this time journal feature of Coach's Plan to make intelligent decisions about which projects to accept and which to decline.

It's incredible what a little documenting can do to improve your results.

Tomorrow

This is the final section, and Coach leaves it blank for Next-Day You to fill it in as needed.

Here's how this section works. Any time you are in execution mode and identify something you need to do tomorrow or at some later point, log it in this section and get back to the task at hand.

This includes moments where you recall something you need to do that you forgot to document, and new action items that pop up along the way. This also includes those instances where you realize you aren't going to have time to complete a task and you need to push that item from the "If there's time" column of today's To Do list to tomorrow.

The Planning & Execution Cycle

We've covered what to include in your plan, so now it's time to talk about the cycle of planning and execution. This won't take long. It's simple.

At some point after Next-Day You completes execution for the day, it's time for Coach to step in and reflect on the day.

How did it go? What did you accomplish? What did you learn about your personal process? What worked? What didn't?

Remember that you documented these thoughts as they came to you in the Process Observations section. This is your opportunity to reread, digest, and think about the best way to incorporate that feedback into your next plan.

After that, you write your plan for the next day.

When you wake up the next day, you execute on Coach's Plan.

That's it.

On-the-Fly Adjustments

No battle plan survives first contact with the enemy. At least, that's what I've heard. I've never been in anything but a metaphorical battle.

The same principle applies to Coach's Plan. The schedule you craft isn't always going to hold up.

Curveballs hit you. Last-minute meetings get scheduled. Urgent tasks pop up. You need to adapt on the fly.

This is the most delicate aspect when it comes to proper execution of Coach's Plan. The one thing we do not want to do is to open the door for the all-star player and master of execution to start tampering with Coach's Plan. That's not the player's job. That's a habit we're trying to change. We want to eliminate the possibility of motivation levels, willpower, mood, and so forth from dictating how you spend your time and what decisions you make.

Here's how we manage this:

First, we only ever adjust Coach's Plan when there's a true need. "True need" means there's a real curveball that will result in consequences if you don't adjust your plan to address it.

Here are a few things that do not constitute real needs:
- Realizing your plan could be better if you made one little change.
- Wishing you remembered to include time for something.
- Feeling too tired.
- Not being in the right headspace for a task.

Even if you are one hundred percent confident the adjustment you want to make is a positive one, if it isn't because of a true need, you must avoid the temptation. It's unsanctioned tampering. Unsanctioned tampering is a huge no-no.

Treat Coach's Plan as sacred, despite any weaknesses you encounter along the way. Trust the plan. Follow the plan.

Remember that within a short period of time, the weaknesses in your plans become few and far between because of the iterative nature of your daily feedback loop. You can confirm this by your decreasing use of the Process Observations section over time.

Also, remember that the worst price you would pay if Coach handed you a terrible plan is wasting one day. After that, there's a reset. Of course, Coach doesn't actually create terrible plans that waste an entire day in real life. This is more of an excuse your mind uses to avoid diving in and embracing the Coach's Plan system.

It's also helpful to remind yourself that unsanctioned tampering nets out negatively for you in the long run. For every positive unsanctioned adjustment, you will make more than one negative unsanctioned adjustment. This is the physics of mood-based and preference-based decision making.

Not only that, but you give Coach's Plan its power by treating it as sacred. It becomes your secret weapon for tackling just about any task or personal change, because any time you write something into a plan, you *know* it's going to happen. That's a powerful place to be as a human, and it's something very few people enjoy.

So, build the habit of surrendering to the plan, even when you spot something suboptimal. That small habit will turn you into a superhero.

When you do recognize a true need for making sanctioned adjustments to your plan, the best technique is as follows:

Stop what you're doing, put on Coach's hat, and take a couple of minutes to quickly adjust your plan *for the rest of the day* based on the new requirements. Make sure you now have a plan you can follow for the rest of the day without any further adjustments required.

After that, forget about it, step back into the role of the all-star player, and get back to execution.

What if another true need for a game-time adjustment pops up later in the day?

Repeat the same process.

This becomes second nature in time, especially as you build your experience writing daily plans. The whole adjustment process takes a couple of minutes. For most people, it's rare for a curveball to completely upend their day. Usually, it's a matter of adjusting some of the timing associated with your tasks.

When I use a paper notebook for Coach's Plan, my schedule forms a column on the left half of the page. As I execute the plan, I place checkmarks by the items I follow as planned. When I adjust the schedule because of a true need, most of the time all I need to do is scribble out times and update them with new ones. When changes are more substantial, I cross out the items on the left column and create an updated version of my schedule on the right side of the page.

You can do this any way that works best for you. The key is to quickly replan the rest of your productive time right then and there, and then take Coach's hat off and get back to executing the plan without question or hesitation.

Some Quick Advice

Now you know the fundamental architecture of Coach's Plan. I have two pieces of advice to offer you. My first piece of advice is this:

Start with mine, then make it yours.

By "start with mine," I mean follow the description I gave you for Coach's Plan to the letter for the first day or two.

By "make it yours," I mean exactly that. Coach's Plan is meant to be adaptive. Learn what works best for you in terms of helping improve your performance and well-being and adjust your use of the Coach's Plan approach accordingly.

Change the categories I outlined or give them names that you prefer. Experiment with different ways of implementing the process. But stay true to the most important elements of Coach's Plan, which I see as the following:
- Create your plan for tomorrow *today*.
- Write out a schedule for all your productive time.
- Write down your observations about your personal process as you execute the plan and use that learning to improve the schedules and plans you write.

- Follow your plan to the letter and only make sanctioned game-time adjustments.

My second piece of advice is this:

Try Coach's Plan for an entire week. This gives you some time to get into a rhythm with it and gauge its potential in your life. In my own case, I noticed some stunning outcomes within the first couple of days.

I'm nearly ready to set you loose. But before I do, I want to share some secrets with you about getting the most from Coach's Plan.

Here we go.

Trust Coach's Plan

In this chapter, I share every one of my secrets about extracting the greatest value from Coach's Plan. These are the secrets I have discovered so far, and because I'm always learning, I'm always adding to this list.

Keep track of the secrets you discover and add them to your own list. Then share them with the world so we can unleash an army of people doing amazing things at higher output and with greater mojo than anyone who has ever walked the planet.

Or keep the secrets to yourself and use them to your own advantage. Your call. I don't judge.

Trust Coach's Plan

There is no tip more important than this:

Trust Coach's Plan.

Allow this to become your mantra. Repeat it to yourself early and often.

"Trust Coach's Plan" means that you place your complete trust in the plan you created as Coach on any given day and execute it to the absolute best of your ability. Throw yourself into it one hundred percent.

That doesn't mean struggle, push, stress, fight, and exhaust yourself with extreme effort. It means relax into the schedule and follow it. Ignore the urges to go off-script.

For this productivity and personal change system to have its full power and potency, you need to give yourself fully to the plan you lay out for yourself each day. The more you switch off that part of yourself that reflects, judges, and narrates, and simply follow the plan, the more success you experience.

The more success you experience, the more faith you have in Coach's wisdom and the more willing you become to follow the plan to the letter to the best of your ability. It's a self-reinforcing loop.

Over time, you naturally expand Coach's tasks. You find yourself tackling harder challenges, like ingrained habits you previously thought of as too difficult to change. You become the best version of yourself without the struggle you're accustomed to feeling when making those changes.

This only happens if you trust Coach's Plan. You only reap these benefits if you treat Coach's Plan as sacred on the days you use this approach.

I mentioned this point earlier, but I want to reiterate it because of how critical it is. If you trust Coach's Plan, it becomes your secret weapon for accomplishing incredible things. You can take some of the thorniest, most entrenched personal struggles you face, and simply by writing a set of actions into your plan, you *know* you are going to effect the change you seek. You imbued Coach's Plan with this power by treating it as sacred and committing one hundred percent to following it on any given day you are using this system.

TRUST COACH'S PLAN

But if you don't treat Coach's Plan as sacred by trusting it and following a plan to the letter to the best of your ability, you disempower the system and yourself in the process.

Think about it this way:

If you cut some corners and ignore 10% of your plan, what's stopping you from ignoring 20% the next day and 30% the day after that?

Within a short period of time, you won't experience any better results on a day you're using Coach's Plan than any other day. You'll be one of the people who says, "Nope, Coach's Plan didn't work for me."

The system isn't a silver bullet. There's no such thing as silver bullets in life.

You are the one who imbues the system with its power. In turn, the system amplifies this power and gives it back to you in spades. You can only imbue it with power if you treat it as sacred and trust Coach's Plan fully on the days you employ this system.

It doesn't take long for your trust in this system to grow organically from watching what it does to your life.

But early on, it can be helpful to remind yourself of a couple things.

If you're deeply skeptical and you still harbor doubts about switching off game-time adjustments, remind yourself that the worst thing that can happen if you follow a suboptimal plan is that you waste one day. Even that day isn't a true waste because you learn from the experience, and you don't make the same planning mistakes again.

Also, you can use a little technique I've found helpful. When I'm done crafting a plan, I look it over and ask myself,

"If I follow this plan to the letter, will tomorrow be a success?"

The answer is always *yes*.

The reason is because Coach is essentially my higher self. Knowing this makes it easier to set questions aside and simply follow the prescription for a successful day that Coach defined the day before.

The final reminder I've found helpful is to reflect on the fact that I've never reached the end of a day when I've followed Coach's Plan to the letter and felt regret. That day is always a win, by definition, regardless of results.

That sounds like a bold claim. Why can I say that with such confidence?

That brings me to the next important secret of this approach.

Process, Not Outcomes

Study the highest performers in any field, and you discover a crucial fact. The best of the best are process-focused, not outcomes-focused.

There's an obvious reason for this. They aren't bleeding energy by focusing on what they can't control, so all their energy is channeled into what they can control. This is one of the key factors fueling their outstanding performance.

All you can ever control is your process. All you can do is put in the work, do the training, and channel your effort into getting better.

Results flow from process. But there is never perfect correlation between process and results. There are always going to be uncontrollable elements that impact the outcome.

Spending any of your effort trying to control what is uncontrollable is a waste of time and energy that you can otherwise pour into mastering your process.

Likewise, spending any mental energy lamenting unwanted outcomes—especially when you nailed the process—is fool's business.

All you can ever control is your process.

This mindset is also the key to true well-being. Want to eliminate a significant portion of your stress in life?

Let go of outcomes and focus on process.

There's a line in the *Tao Te Ching* I have quoted more times than almost any other piece of wisdom. It reflects this point I'm making, and it makes an incredible mantra as well:

> *Do your work, then step back… the only path to serenity.*

When it comes to implementing Coach's Plan in your life, here is the true definition of success:

You followed Coach's Plan to the letter to the absolute best of your ability on any given day you used the system.

That is a win. That is a day you can be proud of.

If you don't get the results you want, it doesn't matter.

In fact, even if you completely failed on every dimension as measured by results, *you* didn't fail. The *plan* failed. You still succeeded, because you spent one more day brilliantly training in becoming an action-oriented master executor.

Process, not outcomes.

Trust Coach's Plan. Be the master executor.

Stopping Mid-Stream

To be the master executor, you must learn how to follow your schedule as precisely as possible.

The way I like to do this is to set a countdown timer at the beginning of a block of time that dings at the end of that block of time. That way I never have to watch the clock during a block of my schedule, and I never accidentally run over my allotted time window.

I have used the native countdown timer on my phone, a free online countdown timer I found through a quick internet search, and a cheap kitchen timer. Sometimes I like to see how much time I have remaining; other times that doesn't matter. Sometimes I need something portable; other times I'm at my computer, so anything will do.

As the master executor, you're often going to be faced with a specific situation: the timer beeps, but you're still in the middle of your task. You may not feel inclined to stop working on that task mid-stream.

You may even be in the groove of a lifetime, with genius flowing from your every pore. The last thing you're going to want to do in that situation is to stop.

But you are a master executor, and you trust Coach's Plan. Stop anyway. Stop right in the middle of a task.

It may be uncomfortable at first. Build that new muscle. Become the master executor. Follow your plan as precisely as possible. Don't succumb to an urge to make an unsanctioned game-time adjustment.

In my own case, I allow a five-minute buffer in either direction at the end of a time window. If I stop a few minutes early to get some water, I still consider this following my plan to the letter. If I end a few minutes late to allow myself to get to a slightly better stopping point on a task, I still consider this following my plan to the letter.

There is only one exception I make to the rule of always stopping mid-stream within the five-minute buffer.

If I'm working on something that is mandatory that I complete that day and I realize I didn't budget enough time to complete it, this represents the need for a sanctioned game-time adjustment.

When this happens, I take off the player hat, reshuffle the rest of the day's plan as Coach, and resume as the master executor.

Otherwise, I stop mid-stream all the time, and it's essential for you to do the same. Trust Coach's Plan.

Sometimes, everything inside me is screaming, "Go off-script, Mike! You're cranking on this task, and it will feel so good to get it done!"

But that's not a sanctioned adjustment. The physics of mood-based decision-making applies here. I always end up with net-negative results when I go off-script. I always feel better at the end of the day when I follow Coach's Plan. And over any length of time, my results show for it too. This is what it means to master your personal process.

The more you practice stopping and switching, the better you become at it. You also come to trust your ability to get into the groove, and you're likely to experience gains in your ability to move into flow states more efficiently.

Since following Coach's Plan, my ability to move into flow states has improved exponentially. I no longer fear stopping mid-stream because I know that the peak state of performance I may be experiencing in that moment is only ever an arm's length away.

Trust Coach's Plan. Stop mid-stream.

Fitting the Container

Parkinson's Law tells us that the work expands to fill the time we allot.

The corollary is also true: the work tends to contract to fit within the time window we give it.

Implement Coach's Plan and witness for yourself the truth of this. This is another embedded secret weapon of this powerful personal productivity system.

It's amazing what happens when you decide how long certain tasks should take, schedule them for that length of time, and then execute with the intention of completing them in that time.

You spin your wheels less. You don't waste time on the trivial. You trim off the fat. You find a way to get it done.

Rarely does your quality suffer. You make good decisions. Anything you didn't do likely wasn't essential anyway.

The work doesn't expand because you gave it an appropriate container and you are a master executor.

Day-Tight Compartments

One of the ways human beings notoriously bleed precious psychic energy is by allowing their headspace to become too occupied by past and future.

Coach's Plan is an excellent antidote to this because of its focus on *one day at a time.*

I commandeered and repurposed a phrase coined by Dale Carnegie, as it serves as an excellent mantra for the Coach's Plan mentality:

> *Live in day-tight compartments.*

Days are the perfect fundamental unit of measurement from a productivity and personal well-being standpoint. When you truly learn to live one day at a time, you are healthier and more effective. This mentality focuses you on the only thing you can control—how you live today—and it subordinates the past and future to secondary roles, which is exactly where they belong.

There's a reason "one day at a time" is a fundamental principle guiding 12-step recovery programs. Day-tight compartments are foundational to habit change, and 12-step recovery programs focus on addressing one of the most entrenched and difficult behavioral changes there is for a person to make.

All too often, we get ahead of ourselves. We look too far into the future and focus on an abstract end goal. This tendency is disempowering, and it frequently overwhelms us.

Life isn't lived in the crossing of finish lines. Crossing finish lines are tiny blips on the overall canvas of your life. Besides, cross one finish line, and you immediately replace it with a new one anyway.

Life is lived day-to-day, moment-to-moment. It's lived in the process. It's lived in the journey. Destinations only ever turn out to be waypoints on a broader journey.

There is a place for long-term planning. But make your long-term plan, then set it aside and focus on today. Revisit your long-term plan periodically, but don't live in your plans.

Likewise, look backwards periodically to enjoy your successes and learn from your failures, but don't live in the past.

Focus on today. Focus on now.

Plan for Focus and Flow

One of the most powerful techniques I have embraced in my life has been training myself in how to move into flow states more efficiently and effectively.

Flow states are periods of deep focus where you feel and perform at your best. They're what athletes refer to as being "in the zone," and they aren't limited to athletic endeavors. Flow states cause you to lose your sense of self and become immersed in the activity of the moment. You lose track of time. You feel energetic, yet relaxed. It's one of the highest states a human can enter.

Training flow states is one of the key lessons in my on-demand video course, *Self-Mastery for Leaders*, precisely because flow states are a hallmark of peak performance and well-being.

Researchers have investigated flow states over the past several decades and have demonstrated that spending more time in flow states drives extraordinary improvements in productivity. People who have learned how to spend more time in flow states are significantly more effective than their peers.

Likewise, flow has an undeniable positive impact on mental and physiological states of well-being.

I won't retread ground I've covered at length elsewhere, except to call attention to the most foundational aspect of incorporating focus and flow states into Coach's Plan.

You need to schedule them. You need a minimum of 90 minutes (and up to a few hours) of uninterrupted, distraction-free time carved out for tasks that lend themselves to getting into a state of flow.

If you want to improve your creative output in dramatic ways, this is the key to success. Schedule the time. Eliminate every possible distraction, including anything that may bombard you on your dozens of electronic devices. Don't let incoming calls, emails, or any other interruptions disrupt this precious time. You will thank yourself.

Like everything with Coach's Plan, experiment with this and learn what works. What is the right length of time for a focused "work sprint" for you? How much time is best to allocate for different types of tasks?

This technique—scheduling blocks of time and the associated training in flow states—was the most pivotal driver for me writing and releasing two books in nine months while simultaneously launching a business. Writing is one of the tasks that I find requires large chunks of dedicated, uninterrupted time for deep focus and creativity.

Make this technique work for you. It is incredible what you can achieve when you become systematic about cultivating creativity, focus, and flow.

Variety is a Valuable Spice

One of the findings revealed to me through my experiments with Coach's Plan is the benefit of incorporating variety into my schedule.

Some tasks require meaningful blocks of time to achieve deep focus and flow, whereas others do not. But all tasks share a common trait:

Given enough time, you hit a point of diminishing returns. Your focus and energy for the task wanes. The quality and quantity of your output suffers.

Some of my most energetic and productive days involve me spending one or two hours on a task, followed by a break, followed by one or two hours on a completely different task, followed by a break, and so on. Sometimes I come back to the same task later in the day. For many tasks, two hours in the morning and two hours in the afternoon yields better results and a happier Mike than four continuous hours on that task.

Varying the nature of my tasks throughout my day breaks things up and exercises different parts of my brain, which keeps me feeling fresh and helps prevent energy lulls.

This is also a useful way for me to follow through on tackling uncomfortable and difficult tasks. Rather than slogging through a task for hours on end or putting myself in situations where I need to re-motivate myself to dive back into something I'd prefer to avoid, I allocate a short period of time to that task and follow it up with a more enjoyable task. Sometimes I repeat this approach throughout the day. It's a lot easier to charge forward on uncomfortable tasks when you know it's going to be a quick sprint and you get to move to something you look forward to doing as soon as the brief time window is up.

Incorporating variety in this way requires that you build the muscle of stopping mid-stream that I mentioned earlier. When you are in the groove on a task, it can feel counterintuitive to stop—especially if it's a task you need to complete or to make significant progress on that day.

But this is where Coach's Plan helps you see things from a bigger picture.

If breaking things up and building in variety boosts your overall energy and well-being, allows you to attack tasks with zest, and even arms you with a high success rate in charging through uncomfortable tasks, then the net benefits outweigh the costs of occasionally stopping a task earlier than you'd like.

The way I think about this situation is as follows:

Michael Jordan retired from playing basketball when he was still a threat. Jerry Seinfeld ended the television series *Seinfeld* when ratings and viewership were as high as ever.

We're not even talking about permanent retirement for your task. Why not temporarily retire it on a high?

Scheduling Space

Building space into your schedule is another best practice when it comes to implementing Coach's Plan.

Space for what?

Space for breaks and space for thinking.

Let's start with space for breaks. If you follow your plan to the letter and you don't build in time for breaks, you won't take breaks. Breaks are crucial for well-being and for performance.

Simple enough. Now let's move to space for thinking.

Abraham Lincoln said, "Give me six hours to chop down a tree and I will spend the first four sharpening the axe." Space for thinking is the equivalent of sharpening the axe. The thinking saves you time in the end because it keeps you from slipping into stretches of autopilot where your efforts aren't yielding the maximum return.

We all do it. We focus on the wrong things, or we fail to identify the creative solution capable of reducing the effort required to reach the same goal.

Space for thinking is our greatest weapon against this.

In my work with leaders, it's common for me to hear people complain, "I don't have time to do the long-term planning and strategy work only I can do," or "I don't even have time to think." It's not unusual for busy executives to move from meeting to meeting, to power through mountains of email, and to fight fires all day. Then they reach the end of the day and realize all the important tasks were crowded out by the urgent ones.

The only proven antidote to this is to schedule time for the important work—including space for thinking—and to stick to the schedule.

But most people don't do this. Pretty soon they're like the busy executives running on autopilot, stressed out and frustrated that they haven't found time for the important things that only they can do.

If you want to maximize your productivity, scheduling ample space for breaks and for thinking is crucial. The busier you are, the *more important* these two things become.

I'm reminded of a time where I felt burned out and decided to take two hours every day for meditation and exercise for a full week to regain a sense of mental and emotional balance. I was okay with my productivity taking a hit because I knew I needed this from a personal well-being standpoint.

When the end of the week came, boy did I feel better. And then I looked at my output.

It was outstanding. Surprise!

Experiment. Schedule breaks and space for thinking. See for yourself what happens.

When to Push, When to Back Off

We all have our vices. One of mine is sugar. I like sweet things.

I spent a long time thinking about reducing or eliminating my intake of refined sugar. But this habit change evaded me for some reason.

Then Coach's Plan came along.

The first week I implemented it, I watched as I went several days without resorting to my usual sugar consumption. I was amazed. This aspirational change that previously evaded me happened so easily.

It would have been easy for Coach to keep including "No sugar today" on my list of goals day after day into perpetuity. Luckily, Coach was wiser than that and knew when it was time to back off.

This brings me to a key coaching principle.

When you're wearing the coaching hat, it's important to know when to push and when to back off. Don't build plans every day that require your all-star to constantly perform at peak levels.

It's far better to cycle the intensity of your goals and your schedule than it is to create plans that you don't follow with complete fidelity.

This is no different than the way an intelligent fitness coach goes about training somebody. Sometimes the coach prescribes a high-intensity workout, and other times the coach prescribes a low-intensity workout. Some days are set aside for complete rest and recovery. If you consistently run too high or too low in intensity, your results are suboptimal. A wise workout program includes cycles.

Besides this reality, it's also crucial to remember that what gives Coach's Plan its power for enabling stellar personal productivity and habit formation is the consistency with which you follow it on the days you employ it.

The more you follow your plan for the day, the more your habit of following your plan is reinforced.

The opposite is also true. If you start breaking Coach's Plan, it only makes it easier to break it again the next day. Eventually, you'll throw your hands up and say, "Coach's Plan doesn't work," and go back to the way you used to do things.

The problem isn't with the Coach's Plan system, the problem is usually with Coach. Don't be a terrible coach to yourself.

Allow the intensity of your plans to cycle. Reduce your intensity after a period of pushing. Listen and feel for when you need a day to back off.

This goes for your use of Coach's Plan itself. If you need a completely unscheduled day, set the Coach's Plan system aside and come back to it.

In my personal experience, part of the power of Coach's Plan comes from the fact that I don't use it every single day. When I do, I follow it and it works. Days off from Coach's Plan make it easier to stay committed and follow the plan on the days I'm using it.

Embrace the wisdom of balance and cycles.

Using Coach's Plan as a Reset

I use the Coach's Plan system a lot, but not always.

Sometimes, I consciously decide to take a day or two off from Coach's Plan, either because I sense the need for a break, or because I see that unscheduled days have a different kind of value than days that are completely scheduled. It's helpful to incorporate both into my life.

But sometimes, I inadvertently slip out of the Coach's Plan habit. Over time, I tend to notice my productivity and well-being declining. There is no question that my output and my mental and physical health are superior when I'm consistently using Coach's Plan.

As compelling as that is, even that isn't enough to prevent my human tendencies from sometimes winning out. As with everybody, I go through cycles of ups and downs.

One thing I have seen to be the case is that if I go through a slump of any kind—low mood, low productivity, low self-care, you name it—and if I haven't been using Coach's Plan at that time, then Coach's Plan serves as an incredible reset button to get me back on track toward high productivity and total well-being.

The same may be true for you. Give it a try and see for yourself.

Witness the Benefits. Grok Them.

My final recommendation for getting the most out of Coach's Plan is to implement it in your life, pay careful attention to the benefits, write them down, and grok them. The more you deeply internalize the benefits, the more Coach's Plan becomes a self-reinforcing habit that further elevates you to new levels of output and well-being.

I have experienced so many benefits since Coach's Plan came into my life, and many of them were unexpected.

There's a maxim that goes, "Do what's hard and life gets easy."

TRUST COACH'S PLAN

Coach's Plan is a system for making this truth a reality in your life. It removes much of the perceived difficulty behind doing what we typically think of as hard. You don't have to do what's hard; you simply have to stick to Coach's Plan. It doesn't take that much effort to "do what's hard" in this case because all you have to do is follow what Coach expertly laid out for you. Most days, doing this turns out to be a joy.

It's a paradox, but this structure provides freedom. Removing decision-making from execution reduces mental spinning and overall effort exerted.

The results speak for themselves.

High quality output. Habit change. Ease. Mojo.

Witness the benefits yourself. Grok them.

You, The All-Star

You have an all-star in you. Perhaps you already enjoy outstanding levels of performance and well-being. Even so, there's untapped potential in you. There always is.

Where's the upper limit of this potential?

What goals have you yet to accomplish because they've been too large to tackle?

What habits have you yet to change because they've been too thorny and ingrained?

What levels of mental and physical well-being are possible for you to reach?

Are you curious to find out?

Well, Coach, it's time to build your plan.

Uncommon Acknowledgments

There are many people I could thank at the end of this book, but I just want to thank one:

You.

Thank you for reading this short manual. I hope it has an outsized impact in your life. I hope it triggers something incredible in you that neither of us expected.

If you think this manual has the potential to help somebody you know, please tell them about it. I would also be tremendously grateful if you took the time to review it. It makes a huge difference to a person who is still early in his journey of stepping out on his own.

If you enjoyed this and are curious about any of the other things I've put into this world, or the work I do for individuals and organizations, or you are simply interested in connecting with me, you can find all of your answers in one place at www.mikekav.com.

Thank you for being awesome.

Also by Mike Kavanagh

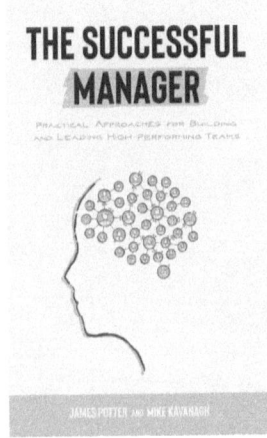

Additional Free and Premium Content

New Book Releases
Online Courses
Podcast & Videos
Newsletter
Visit www.mikekav.com

www.ingramcontent.com/pod-product-compliance
Lightning Source LLC
Chambersburg PA
CBHW031542210526
45464CB00003B/1111